Denise M. Baran-Unland's Irish Genealogy

By Edward Calkins

Copyright © 2017 by Denise M. Baran-Unland
All rights reserved. No part of this book may be
reproduced, scanned, or distributed in any printed or
electronic form without permission.
Printed in the United States of America
ISBN: 13: 978-0-9983134-9-8

This book is lovingly dedicated to the reader, whoever you might be.

"It's true that I'm a ham. But I also believe that good cheer is contagious."
- **Edward Calkins, Steward of Tara**

TABLE OF CONTENTS

Introduction

Chapter 1: Uly's News

Chapter 2: A Homer Run for Uly

Chapter: 3: Leo the Comic

Chapter 4: Leo the Christian

Chapter 5: Leo and the Lions

Chapter 6: The Irish Heresies

Chapter 7: Brother Clover

Chapter 8: Religious War

Chapter 9: Double Checked

Chapter 10: Not Just The Tip

Chapter 11: Triple Agent

Chapter 12: Boxer Poet

Chapter 13: Irish Shuffle

Twenty Questions with Ed Calkins

Biographies

INTRODUCTION

In Bryony, the first book of Denise M. Baran-Unland's supernatural/literary BryonySeries, protagonist Melissa Marchellis meets one vampire who stands apart from the Victorian society in which she travels with composer and pianist John Simons.

That vampire is Ed Calkins, who calls himself, "The Steward of Tara." And Ed is also a real person.

Ed believes that it is the right of every Irishman to create myth. Under this premise, Ed became a vampire. He also penned my "Irish" genealogy.

This genealogy first appeared in serial installments on the BryonySeries blog in late 2010 and early 2011. It's reprinted for you today.

Enjoy!

CHAPTER ONE: ULY'S NEWS

Although Denise's Irish ancestry cannot be directly proven, it's quite apparent to any rational being that lacks prejudices to the contrary.

Denise's first known ancestor is a man named "Uly of Too Many Children." He was smallish man, studious, numerant, and, if eye glasses had been invented before 1700 B.C. and available along the eastern Mediterranean coast, he would have worn very thin lenses.

Uly married a woman to whom he never paid much attention since he favored scrolls and theroms to her feminine charms. Nonetheless, she bore sixteen children, none of which were fathered by Uly. So Uly, after Number 16, (which was actually the child's name because Uly was very good with numbers, but had trouble with names and complex sentence structures, although he was very good with complex equations) realized that his wife had been cheating! As he prepared to throw her out, it suddenly occurred to him that she had been gone for several months.

Anyway, poor Uly and his sixteen unknown children were left to fend for themselves. What did Uly do? He took a paper route by ocean. Because this was three thousand years before the invention of the printing press, a carrier in Uly's time had to compose the paper first, copy it as many times as he had customers, then deliver it. One could say that Uly was a publisher, reporter, and carrier. The route consisted of the ancient equivalent of a trailer court and gated community.

Each morning, Uly would compile his observations of the following day, write them on a scroll, and give it to the lowest numbered child to replicate. That child would give his copy to the child whose number was one less than his until all children were copying and all editions were written.

Uly had two publications to deliver: The Hellenic Times and the Trojan Inquirer. Each bore the same news, but the trailer court, which preferred the Hellenic Times, and the gated community which received the Trojan Inquirer, were none the wiser.

In addition, it might be added that the children quickly grew bored of their copying tasks. Sometimes, bored with journalistic integrity and ready at any chance to rebel against parental authority, they wrote their own views instead of Uly's representations of the facts. Others drew comedic pictures. In this way, Uly's papers might have invented the editorial and the political cartoon.

CHAPTER TWO: A HOMER RUN FOR ULY

Uly and his sixteen children continued their newspaper business for many years until one day, someone from the trailer court approached Uly and said, "Hey buddy, are you going to deliver in Troy next? Could ya do me a favor and take this wooden horse with you? I forgot the keypad code to do it myself."

Uly agreed. I think you know where this is going.

What you don't know is that the sounds of the sacking of Troy woke Uly up from his afternoon nap. He could hear the shouts and see the smoking towers. Grabbing a pad of paper, he rushed into the burning city to get the full story. Hoping to get some interviews for a human-interest angle, he busted a burning door and ran up a flight of smoking stairs.

There in the doorway was the most beautiful woman in the world. So stunned by her grace, wit, and fashion-forward sensibilities, he began to compose poetry. So seduced by his lyrical praise, she blushed, felt faint, and could produce not a word of protest.

Despite their awkward first meeting, Uly, who lost his route the very next day, took Helen of Troy back with him to Greece, along with her fourteen named children and his sixteen numbered children. They had a child together on that journey home, thus naming him Homer. The other thirty children felt a little envious of the youngest child whom both parents called the same way.

As for the numbered children, whom Helen never numbered, and the named children of whom Uly could never pronounce their names they might be excused for occasionally misrepresent-ting themselves to parents, community, history, and Homer himself. It therefore cannot be ruled out that the Great Homer, author of those famous poems, was fathered by an Irishman.

Moreover, it must be said that the great Homer was not the only great man who bore the name. There was Homer, the Roman gladiator, who was handed only a club in his first bout. With one blow, he knocked off the head of his opponent and sent it soaring into the stands, thus inventing a brand-new sport still played today.

CHAPTER THREE: LEO THE COMIC

Leo the Comic lived somewhere in Greece during the first century and was likely the first Christian in Denise's blood line. However, he wasn't very successful as a Christian after being told many times that the only way he'd get to heaven was martyrdom. It seems that, although Leo was kind hearted, he was very weak-willed.

By the age of ten, he was begging in front of bakeries for the funds to eat the delicacies inside. People thought this hysterical and dropped coins in his cup to pay for the laugh. Later, comic book shops added to his obsessions, as did his value as comic relief. Worse for Leo, the Greco-Roman community was in denial about Leo's condition, believing, despite the evidence, that Leo was just acting out for a laugh.

By the age of twenty, Leo knew that his life was running afoul. The comic books and doughnuts were killing him. Worst of all, the city loved him, thinking his compulsive behavior made him the best humorist that Greece had ever known. Back then, there were no 12- step programs to help him, so Leo turned to the newly outlawed religion.

The small Christian community did its best to save poor Leo. In the early Eastern Church, it was well-known not to be in line behind Leo at the confessional. Deeply worried for Leo's soul, the local priest decided to use tough love to purge the addictions. He commanded Leo to spend one day kneeling on rice in the underground church for every doughnut he ate and comic book he purchased.

After six years of kneeling, Leo's behavior started to change. When Leo failed to show up at any bakeries or comic book shops as the secret Christian spies had reported, the priest was ready to claim Leo sin-free. Instead, it came out that Leo kicked the doughnut habit by stuffing himself with the rice, and that he could no longer afford rising cost of comic books. Defeated, the priest suggested Leo try a different religion. That's when Leo decided to take martyrdom seriously.

CHAPTER FOUR: LEO THE CHRISTIAN

By now, a life of compulsion had taken its toll. Already very overweight, hopelessly in debt, over thirty, and unable to find any really good comic books; how much did Leo really have to lose? Nero had already died, and with each new emperor, the Christian persecutions had expanded. Each day the coliseum's scratch sheet listed the deaths of Christian inmates as a "sure bet." Why couldn't he get in on that?

The next day, Leo stood in the center of the town square and proclaimed himself a Christian. The townsfolk doubled over with laughter. Leo insisted, revealing the cross he wore under his tunic around his neck. They laughed even harder, tossed coins in his direction, and swore that this comic prop was even better than the doughnut- stained scratch sheet he once produced when he did that bit about being "addicted." The more he insisted, the harder they laughed, catapulting his comedian career while dooming his ambitions as a martyr.

In the days that followed, Leo's professing to being Christian began competing with coliseum attendance, creating an ancient version of late night TV wars. No matter what he tried, Leo's proclamations of Christianity were the most outrageous jokes to grace the streets. Not helpful was Leo's new addiction. No longer able to afford comic books, Leo discovered that the images in temples were far more entertaining and enjoyable than kneeling on rice. Perhaps the best joke passed around was him claiming he only went to temples for the art! Even his habit of wearing a white tunic with a red cross only got him the called "The Comic Crusader". (I wonder if Leo invited the T Shirt.) After years of this, Leo realized he would never make martyrdom.

Finally, Leo, now morbidly obese and spiritually devastated, gave in to the priest and converted to Hinduism, which required a diet of only vegetables. Perhaps it was the change of diet, but Leo's addictive personality began to withdraw. Not only did he avoid bakeries, and kneeing on rice, but he stopped proclaiming, which destroyed his career as a comedian. In addition, he lost a lot of weight which didn't escape the local military. It occurred to the authorities that

Leo was fasting, and probably kneeing on rice in secret. The authorities, who never really enjoyed humor, realized it first. Leo was a Christian!

Crowds gathered at his home when he was arrested, convinced that this was a comic stunt that the government was in on. They roared, rolled, and choked with laughter as Leo loudly protested that he was no longer Christian.

CHAPTER FIVE: LEO AND THE LIONS

Then came the day at the coliseum when Leo was to be fed to the lions. In the stands was a man known only as The Donald, who once controlled all the coliseum betting in the Roman empire and had just sold half his business to the Roman government.

The Donald loved to gamble, but he hated to leave things to chance. He had good reason to be confident that no matter how many Christians the lions ate, he would make money. What he didn't count on was the worst relapse in history.

Modern 12- step programs tell you "every slip has a start." For Leo, it was a small wager he placed while being dragged to his trial. "Five on the lions," he called. But through the shouting the bookie heard, "Five on Leo," and so the bet was booked.

Now, after six years of no red meat, no salt, only healthy rabbit's food, Leo saw the hungry lions and saw only red meat. The carnage that occurred broke the bookies, angered animal activists, and devastated Leo's low calorie, low sodium diet. Lions ran in terror as Leo tore limbs to gorge on the red meat. Donald wasn't concerned about the bets on Leo because of the spread. If a better took the lions, he had to spot sixteen Christians.

Donald knew the lions were never fed more than ten. After ten Christians, the lions wouldn't be hungry. How would it look to the coliseum goers if the lions wouldn't eat their daily Christians? On the others side, a better on Christians had to spot two lions. Surely Leo would stop eating after one. The Donald had no idea what it's like eating lettuce for six years. In a public display of morbid gluttony, Leo didn't stop eating till the last lion in Greece was consumed.

After this, Donald was still smiling. You see, he had sold half his bookie operations to the Roman government. Now they would find out which half they got! (Collection, Donald/Payouts, Rome) Some say that this debt caused the fall of Rome. For his additional offence of animal cruelty, Leo was banished from the Roman Empire, and so his story ends in the Latin Chronicles without a word of where he went.

Consider where Leo could have gone after banishment. Would he have gone to southern Africa? After eating as many lions, I would think that Leo would avoid that temptation, don't you? Is not it more likely that he would have gone as far from lions as he could get...as in north....but not within the Roman Empire? I think you get my point.

CHAPTER SIX: THE IRISH HERESIES

This chapter of Denise's ancestors has the chance meeting of two people who never knew they were related. To understand this meeting, one must partake in a little Irish history. We must go to the seventh century where a young Bishop, who REALLY didn't like snakes, waited in a vestibule from the Vatican for permission for his proposed trip back to the island that enslaved him years before. Finally, the answer came to Patrick, still in the vestibule but now twenty years older, that he could go. (These things take time.) Many of you know this story. In a few years, not only was Patrick's mission accomplished, (killing all the snakes), but the Irish people were converted as well.

Not long afterwards, the Vatican wished they had stayed pagan. You see, even though the church grew, abbeys were formed, and priests were consecrated, swelling the number of followers under its power, two traits of the Irish clergy began to emerge. First, the Irish took to writing in Latin with passion and a brogue. Very quickly papers on church doctrine flowed southeast at alarming rates, making monasteries around the world wondering if the printing press had been invented early. But more damaging, the Irish tended to make things up.

Of course, Rome had dealt with heresies before, but the stuff coming from the Irish had a certain charm, making theologians wish they had come up with it themselves. Besides that, they couldn't match the volume of myths and superstitions enough to call them out, such as the doctrine of "White Martyrdom", (a concept that sounds suspiciously like Leo the Comic's situation.)

The idea went like this. Since Ireland was outside of the Roman Empire during the 300 years of Christian persecutions, other nationalities had an unfair advantage of going to heaven. Surely God wanted more Irishmen up there with Him. So, as a spiritual affirmative action program' aimed at an ethnically diverse heaven; the "White Martyrdom" program recognized that it's hard to die for one's faith if no one will kill you. Instead, one could abandon civilization, go off to some wilderness, practice the common religious extremities, and enjoy a full martyrdom state without the blood or death. Sensing the bargain, Irish everywhere began searching for harsh, uninhabitable places and building communities there. I should state here that it is completely untrue that New York and Chicago were founded this way.

CHAPTER SEVEN: BROTHER CLOVER

To such an end, Brother Clover and his fellow monks discovered an unpopulated shore of ice somewhere in the northwestern Atlantic and pledged to eke out a living there. Lest that prove too easy, they also took vows of chastity, poverty, and silence.

Not long afterwards, boats appeared on the horizon. More brothers wanted in on this. Unwilling to horde their spiritual riches, the brothers accepted the new recruits but added more prayer and longer work days to the docket.

As years went by, more monks came to join, to the point where the island, harsh as it was, became quite populated, some would say crowded, so vegetarianism was added. (More evidence that Clover was related to Leo the Comic.) This did stop the less committed from becoming monks, but it didn't stop them from wanting to serve God, through helping the monks.

It started innocently enough, an occasional cake baked from someone's mother, but it rapidly expanded. Soon, mothers fought over the right to cook for the monks, while gardeners competed to work in the gardens. Dishes got washed. Clothes were pressed. Furniture was dusted. Even people without time to help this way insisted on getting a piece of the martyr racket by tossing coins on the shore. Monks became so fat and lazy they could hardly walk.

   Brother Clover could take no more. In a combination of miming, finger gesturing, and mouthing words, he laid down the law. No servants for the monks! They all had to leave and take their meals, clothes, furniture, perfumes, footbaths, fine art, pinball machines, jewels, fineries, and money with them! Well, the monks understood perfectly but their mothers refused to get the hint.

CHAPTER EIGHT: RELIGIOUS WAR

Luckily, help was to come from Rome. There, a certain visionary ability for predicting future trends was not matched with basic knowledge of geography or common sense. Cardinal Bush realized that a new religion was gaining converts in the spiritual vacuum in North Africa.

He knew if something wasn't done, this new religion would spread to rival that of the church. Missionaries had to be deployed! Existing orders had to be reinvented. To this end, he sent Brother Clover and his monks a new mandate: "Go to Greece and convert any potential Turks." Shrugging his shoulders, Brother Clover deployed his monks, leaving the island of Iceland to be discovered and settled later in history.

Once in Greece, the flaw of sending a pack of monks, who knew not a word of Greek and taking a vow of silence anyway, became clear. The monks did their best they to pantomime the gossip but the populous, who were already Christian, thought the Catholic guys in ropes were suffering some kind of spastic disorder possibly caused by a misplaced devotion to a pope. Doing what they did back then when anyone had spastic fits, they called the priests for help.

Perhaps this could have been the first Christian vs. Christian religious war as the priests and brothers eyed each other hostilely. Surely bad words would have slipped if the monks could talk. Fists might have flown if they weren't men of the cloth. Angry gestures were directed at the priests and were countered by words in Greek, but both sides quickly realized the futility of this confrontation. Quickly it was decided that a drinking contest was the only way to settle it.

CHAPTER NINE: DOUBLE CHECKED

Now, as luck would have it, the winery down the block was owned by a descendant of Uly of Too Many Children. This is clear because her name was Number Six. Predictably, as in any drinking contest be-tween Irishmen and Greeks, the contest lasted for three days.

Number Six and her staff struggled valiantly to refill the tankers of wine that the holy men consumed with bravo. After three days, however, priests and brothers alike began to collapse in drunken stupors. It's unclear who won. The last man drinking was probably too drunk to know he was alone. Nor could Number Six and her staff be sure, for after the straight days without sleep, they collapsed too (not everyone has the stuff of a news carrier).

What is known is that in the hangover that followed, the monks assumed that they had endured enough misery to claim some derivative of martyrdom, paid the check, and left for Ireland. On the trip back, they began rethinking the retreat from the vows they had taken. Clearly silence and poverty were overrated and, while chastity was a great way to stay single, it wasn't getting anyone any grandchildren.

Unknown to history is whether or not Orthodox priests had the same post-hangover during their rethinking, but it is known that they paid the check.

CHAPTER TEN: NOT JUST THE TIP

Number Six woke the next day to discover that the check for three days drinking, a large fortune by dark age standards, $7 and 43.7 cents by today's money, had been paid twice. Fearing divine retribution, Number Six knew she had to return the halves to the appropriate party. It is certain that the Orthodox Church got its refund but that was because it was down the block from the winery.

If we are to contend that Number Six, who is an ancestor of Denise, went to Ireland and settled there, what proof could we find? Firstly, we know that Ireland was not experiencing a shortage of beer at the time, so if she ever made it there, she would have no reason to leave, but how do we even know that she realized the monks were from Ireland?

However, there is the fact that two years later the Irish GDP had risen to an unprecedented seven dollars and 47 cents. (.3 cents might have been the tip) The percentage of the rise was uncalculatable seeing that for the last ten years the GDP was zero. (Years before it was negative.)

Clearly both Brother Clover and Number Six spent the rest of their days in Ireland.

CHAPTER ELEVEN: TRIPLE AGENT

The most mysterious person in all of Denise's gene pool is her grandmother. Unfortunately, most of the information about her is still highly classified by several governments. I managed to escape with my life and some pretty juicy stories about this remarkable woman. Now, taking the chance that the nations of the world are too focused on another source of leaks across the internet, I'm prepared to tell the story of a woman whose true name is not even known.

Our story begins in a library somewhere in China during the communist revolution. Agent 0007 had just taken out a book "The Art of War" by Tung Sun just before the communists had taken it. A week later she noticed the same book with one phrase deleted. Curiously, she also noticed the library's map of Ireland had a city blocked out.

Through her correspondences with the CIA, she noticed the deleted phase appearing in free world text, but mistranslated and falsely attributed to a Confuses. Agent 0007 became convinced that these three bits of misinformation were being used to cover weaknesses in the communist mind set.

The Irish city deleted for Chinese maps was Limerick. The phase deleted, the deliberately mistranslated from "The Art of War" was, "' sticks and stones can only break bones but poems write names in infamy."

CHAPTER TWELVE: BOXER POET

Agent 0007 spent the best part of the Cold War with an assumed name, with an assumed husband, giving assumed birth to normal children, which included Denise's mother. She used her spare time in secret CIA underground libraries working on her theory of defensive poetry against the communist threat.

The limericks that she constructed were so powerful that she earned her place as among the three greatest writers of Denise's gene pool. (Remember, that includes Homer and Denise herself.) Unfortunately, it would be years before the CIA's Russian network could get these poems written on the men's rooms of the Kremlin. But when they did, the effect was sudden and complete, forcing, for fear of further insult, the communist party to lay down its stronghold on power and democratic election to be held. Fear of the same in China caused it to embrace a capitalist model for its future.

I wish I could include some of the limericks for this book, but I could not break into the cyber vault that contains them along with the floor plans for nuclear missiles, the landing sites of UFO's, and the location of Hoffa's body. Moreover, these limericks are in Russian. I'm afraid we will know extraterrestrial poems before we can utter the first line of 0007's poetry.

Sadly, Denise's grandmother did not live long enough to see her victory over communism bear fruit. Instead, she lived and wrote the journal of her own heartbreaking defeat. You see, during her limerick writing for the CIA, she chanced upon a youth who was being badly bullied. Concerned for his welfare, she attempted to teach him defensive poetry and documented his progress.

CHAPTER THIRTEEN: IRISH SHUFFLE

For fear of lawsuit, 0007 would never identify the boy. In any case, the boy proved completely inept at poetry of any kind, let alone defensive poetry. Giving up, 0007 taught him how to box.

The tragedy was that the boy never did give up on poetry, with the belief that defensive poems would help him defeat his boxing opponents. Time and time again, the young man would win a championship, only to lose it to some unworthy boxer, because he would spout the poem out before the bout and believe the result was already decided.

Often, agent 0007 would meet her protégé in some remote, secret gym and give him another lesson in humility and boxing. Still, the young man would not relent with his pre-boxing match poetry. Soon, 0007 learned a sad side effect of defensive poetry, if it's not used correctly. The boy became delusional and continued to compose poetry and box well into old age.

How do we know 0007 was Irish? Firstly, with her CIA ties, and zeal against communists, my sources suggest that her true last name was McCarty. More than that is the style of boxing her boy showed. Though he never called it that, he used footwork known as the "Irish shuffle".

TWENTY QUESTIONS WITH ED CALKINS

When I first started the BryonySeries blog in 2011, I posted this Q&A with the real Ed Calkins in several installments. We did this interview months before the release of the first book, and it's published here for your enjoyment.

Just to clarify: Ed Calkins is a real person. He really lives somewhere Chicago-ish and was a supervisor for one of the agents when The Herald-News circulation passed from The Sun Times to the Chicago Tribune. I reported to Ed for my Marycrest route.

My attorney drew up the necessary paperwork for Ed to sign off himself. Seriously.

No Ed is not insane, but wonderfully creative. If you want to know Ed, read the novels, for I dutifully scrawled on brown paper wrapping snatches of conversation overheard in passing at the distribution center while Ed handed out papers (or in longer conversations by phone) to weave in real dialogue with the imaginary dialogue and overall character arc.

I also spent much time with him, getting to know his "ruthless dictator" persona, as to accurately portray it. In a wonderful and truly humbling act of trust, Ed did not want to read any drafts; rather, he wanted the experience of his fictional self however I chose to write it, a very literary and legally-bound, "Do with me as you will."

It was marvelously empowering.

PS: I did such a good writerly job with Ed that one day, after Timothy had been out of the distribution center for a year attending Joliet Junior College and working at the Renaissance Center, he offered to help us roll papers one night and ran into Ed.

Ed said something to the effect of, "Wow, I haven't seen you in a long time." Timothy blinked, yes, literally blinked, in surprise, for he had been reading drafts of Staked! as I had chaptered it off and felt as if he'd seen Ed every day.

Any BryonySeries blog post attributed to Ed was really written by Ed. Just so you know.

And now, the interview:

BARAN-UNLAND: Who is the ruthless dictator?

CALKINS: "My son was doing a lot of role playing games, and he was trying to come up with a bard and give him magical powers. I told him there was no need coming up with magical items, because bards are already too powerful, providing they're not trying to seek notoriety for themselves. Ruthless dictators are not afraid to die. They're just afraid of how they'll be remembered. It's not effective to compose a song or a limerick or an epic poem glorifying yourself. You've got to have other people saying it about you. Why not cut the military in half and invent some really good limericks? You can really insult someone into submission."

BARAN-UNLAND: Why did you invent him?

CALKINS: "I was bullied as a boy, so it came from the way I would get back at bullies. I would think something negative about them, because verbalizing it wouldn't go well. In my mind, I called it even. The ruthless dictator really started when I got a ticket running a stop sign when I was delivering newspapers on a really snowy day. If I had stopped, I would never have gotten going again. I really thought the ticket was unfair. As revenge, I picked ten people out of the phone book and thought bad things about them. My wife thought that was pretty corny. Later, I took over the entire town. I didn't have to conquer a nation. It just had to be a place, at least metaphorically. It had to have its own identity."

BARAN-UNLAND: What was your reaction when asked to become part of a vampire novel?

CALKINS: "I was nervous at revealing my ignorance about vampires. I didn't know a lot about it. I worked quickly to remedy it."
BARAN-UNLAND: Why did you accept?

CALKINS: "Immortality, of course. I can't think about myself in everything. I have to think about 1,000 years from now, and if there's going to be a three-day holiday in my name or not. There's a side of me that thinks this could be goofy enough to think this could actually happen."

BARAN-UNLAND: Weren't you afraid of how you might be portrayed?

CALKINS: "No, and a lot of that comes from my survival mechanism as a kid. I learned to play along with the bullies rather than fight them. Part of my comedic outreach is self-deprecating, so it didn't really seem that anything negative could hurt me. The ruthless dictator would say, 'Look, there's no such thing as bad publicity.' King Midas is much better off than King Midas the Second, even though he was portrayed in a bad light, because nobody remembers King Midas the Second."

BARAN-UNLAND: What if fans expect the real Ed Calkins to be similar to the fictional Ed Calkins?

CALKINS: "He is like him. There's just that side of him. He's significant in an offbeat way, enough to where he can claim the stewardship of Tara without blushing."

BARAN-UNLAND: The Irish have no solid vampire legends. How do you feel about being the first, real Irish vampire?

CALKINS: "I think other people will make more of that than I will. Being known as the Steward of Tara is more of a crowning achievement in my mind."

BARAN-UNLAND: Where did your love of Irish lore and history begin?

CALKINS: "It started with my love of history. Then I looked into mythology, and I used to tell my son a lot of tales and legends. When he reached high school, and heard the same thing, my credibility rose in his eyes. One thing I had told him that wasn't really true is that Ireland was always a backwash of European history, unless your interest is war. Then, it is probably true. There were many Irish warriors. It's just they tended to be fodder; they were never fighting for Ireland. Ireland is probably the only place where you get a sense of what pre-Christianity was about, so if you want to know Ireland, just study its myth. Even before I was really into being Irish, I had a disdain for the Roman Empire, which, I think, gave me a bias toward the Irish. In all honesty, I'm American, but my heritage is Irish. It only takes going to Ireland to know that."

BARAN-UNLAND: How did you research your Irish heritage?

CALKINS: "I've read a lot of books. Also, as a college freshman, I got put into an Irish literature course, which I wasn't very interested in it at the time. I'm not one of those people who have forgotten much of what they learned in college. So, it stayed with me all these years in a recessive way. The problem is that I'm very bad with names. The proper study of Irish mythology involves heroes, kings, and saints, in that order. They are alive today through the last names. I just don't know who these people are."

BARAN-UNLAND: When did you begin writing?

CALKINS: "I started with poetry. In the eighth grade, I wrote a poem that resonated a little bit. So, throughout high school, I wrote poetry. I was an editor of the literary magazine and the editor in chief the last year. Something bizarre about me is that I can't finish anything. I have these really organized fantasies, but I'm not a wordsmith. I just lost my hard drive, which means I lost everything I've written for the last twenty years. I should be beside myself, but I'm not, because none of the pieces were really finished

BARAN-UNLAND: What have you written?

CALKINS: "I actually wrote a historical fiction novel when I was in high school. I had a fascination for Hannibal, so I put myself on the other side facing Hannibal's army. I didn't really know how to handle it, but I did write it."

BARAN-UNLAND: How had you shared your writings in the past?

CALKINS: "I posted them. When I was working on my trilogy, someone would send me an email that said, 'Send me your story,' and

I'd send them a few chapters. Then I'd get another email saying, 'That was great. Send me some more.' So, a lot of it was praise-driven. The problem is that twenty years have passed. The protagonist has become darker and the eroticism is no longer interesting, I hate to admit. In my mind, I've reduced the second book to a single, short story. Also, every novel I've written was also an idea for a game. I had done a really good job of writing the games, again not finished. The smallest details completely derail a project for me."

BARAN-UNLAND: How do you overcome writer's block?

CALKINS: "The truth is I don't. My writing block is fear. By the time I do write, it's only because the ideas have been spilling out over and over and over again through my mind, to where it's enough already. The details have become an irritant, so I just sit down and write."

BARAN-UNLAND: What motivates you to compose a limerick?

CALKINS: "I get ticked off, and my mind starts putting lines together. It's different with limericks because I don't have to actually write them. A limerick is not fine art. Because of its structure, a kindergartener is just as good as composing limericks as an adult."

BARAN-UNLAND: Why is legacy important to you?

CALKINS: "I think it's fascinating to me in the same way history is. Think of Sue, the Tyrannosaurus Rex, which lived approximately 25 million years ago and compare that to the 6,000 years of civilization. In the eyes of God, dinosaurs must be a statement of survivability. Humanity is still an experiment in its infancy. When all is said and done, the history of humans is going to be a lot more significant than the bones of a creature, but we're not there yet. We're going to have to start with many things, including being a lot older than 6,000 years. Maybe there won't be an Ed Calkins parade that 6,000 years old, but maybe there will a 1,000 years old Ed Calkins

Day parade, which will create the much larger tradition of there still being parades."

BARAN-UNLAND: How did the idea for Ed Calkins Day parade originate?

CALKINS: "I discovered that my birthday and Valentine's Day had a little conflict when I started dating my wife. The first year I was dating her; we went out and celebrated my February 13th birthday. Guess what happened on the fourteenth? I didn't have a Valentine for her. That offended her at the time. My defense was, 'Come on, it was my birthday.' I guess that's where started. Then I started joking with other people that my birthday should be a national holiday. When you couple that with Lincoln's birthday and the stars aligned in the sky, you can see it was meant to be."

BARAN-UNLAND: You're famous for cookouts, Queen of Christmas contests, candy canes and Santa hat distribution, and pallet jack races. Why host these things?

CALKINS: "Have fun, of course. Distribution centers can be so dreary. If every day is like the last, no one wants to get up.

BARAN-UNLAND: Do you own a kilt?

CALKINS: "I used to, but I gave it away to my brother. It no longer fit, at the waistline. So, currently, I do not have a kilt. They're not cheap. They can cost a couple hundred dollars."

BARAN-UNLAND: For what occasions did you wear it?

CALKINS: "Initially I wore it St. Paddy's day. I wore it the whole day. I was I in newspapers and, yeah, I went to work with it. My wife wouldn't let me do it after I married her. It happened this way. I have a way of not taking care of garments. When I was starting to date her, most of my jeans had holes in them. She takes care of her possessions. That how I knew we were serious when she started washing my clothes. But when a woman starts washing your clothes, she gets to say what get discarded and what gets kept. You know my striped shirts? Those were her idea. My wife now dresses me. I used to dress differently.

BARAN-UNLAND: What are your plans for the BryonySeries blog?

CALKINS: "I'd like to make some myths of my own, but that won't start until the book comes out. I'm thinking it might be fun to add different side stories of the character into the blog, but maybe, too, I might be able to introduce some of the traditional Irish myths. I've been wanting to write something about the interplay of state fairs in Ireland. There were laws concerning them, such as you couldn't arrest anyone during a fair and you could not engage in war. All combat had to be resolved before a fair was scheduled to start. I'd also like to write about the Knights of the Red Branch and maybe some adventure that happens to some of the knights. That's the neat thing about a blog. Speaking from the character, if something doesn't fit, or if there is something else I want to say, I can always come back with, 'I was just joking. Here's what really happened.' I'm very excited about this. I feel I'm getting closer to that three-day holiday."

Denise M. Baran-Unland is the author of the BryonySeries supernatural/literary trilogy for young and new adults, the Adventures of Cornell Dyer chapter book series for grade school children and the Bertrand the Mouse series for young children.

She has six adult children, three adult stepchildren, fourteen total grandchildren, six godchildren, and four cats.

She is the co-founder of WriteOn Joliet and previously taught features writing for a homeschool coop, with the students' work published in the co-op magazine and The Herald-News in Joliet.

Denise blogs daily and is currently the features editor at The Herald-News. To read her feature stories, visit www.theherald-news.com. For more information about Denise's fiction and to follow her on social media, visit www.bryonyseries.com.

Ed Calkins is a real, 60-something, proud of his Irish-heritage computer programmer and amateur writer who has also spent his entire life working in newspaper circulation. Years ago, Calkins invented a "ruthless dictator" alter ego, also known as "The Steward of Tara."

With Calkins' permission, BryonySeries author Denise M. Baran-Unland furthered altered him to create a minor character in "Bryony," making Calkins the first Irish vampire of any significance. Of course, Calkins claims "Bryony" is really all about him, so he's held his own book signings, which he is calls, "The Ed Calkins Tour." There must be some truth in his sentiments, because Calkins' plot importance does grow with each novel in the original BryonySeries trilogy.

Calkins is the author of "Ruthless" (his backstory) and "Denise M. Baran-Unland's Irish Genealogy." He also shares his writings on the BryonySeries blog. Email him at bryonyseries@gmail.com.

www.ingramcontent.com/pod-product-compliance
Lightning Source LLC
Chambersburg PA
CBHW031434040426
42444CB00006B/800